Stars In Your Dreams

Poems From

The Girl With The Star In Her Eye

Elise

Published by New Generation Publishing in 2020

Copyright © Elise 2020

First Edition

The author asserts the moral right under the Copyright, Designs and Patents Act 1988 to be identified as the author of this work.

All Rights reserved. No part of this publication may be reproduced, stored in a retrieval system or transmitted, in any form or by any means without the prior consent of the author, nor be otherwise circulated in any form of binding or cover other than that which it is published and without a similar condition being imposed on the subsequent purchaser.

ISBN
Paperback	978-1-80031-574-7
Hardback	978-1-80031-573-0

www.newgeneration-publishing.com

New Generation Publishing

Old soul, voices stir within your heart

A girl gazing upon the stars

Ancient stories engraved in you

You know all the magic to be true

Come now into the waters and find your destiny

For at last, on these white shores, you shall be free

Desert rose, how your beauty blooms under the sun

Find your courage for our journey has begun

Look deep within my dear

All the answers shall be found here

Fire in your blood, fire in your soul, fire in your heart

You're looking for a match but darling you are the spark

So go onwards dream girl and set the world alight

Keep burning forever even in the darkest night

Echoes of the mountains ripple through me

Earths whispers singing a magic melody

Listen close and listen well

All of the worlds secrets are here to tell

Wisdom of the wise vibrates through the rock

You, yourself are the key that will open any lock

Midnight darkness encases the sky

The girl gazes at the twinkling stars that never die

Breathing gently as if inside a dream

Oh beauty of Earth nothing is as it seems

On this mythical quest you are bound

Live the adventure that once was lost but now is found

All you have been, all you are and all you will ever be

The magic is within you, now write your own story

Now is the time to trust yourself and fly

For you are The Girl With The Star In Her Eye

Waters running deep

Below the surface where you sleep

Floating in the blue depths of this never-ending sea

With an envelope of dreams and a strong heart beat is she

She who sees all that you know,

She who to you has given the seeds that you now sow

Divine feminine roots deep within the Earth

Where all was foretold, your destiny, your lover and your birth

In this enchanted forest of spirits and memories you lose your mind

All that you thought you knew is left behind

Enter the world of mystical creatures and gateways into the unknown

Surrounded by all that is magic and alive you are never alone

Only after you have fully lost yourself into the chaos and serenity of the woodland

Will you finally know yourself and whats more, you will understand

And in that moment under the sparkling lights, they forgot it all

The world fell away as they danced in harmony at the masked ball

Dancing for their life, for their love, to always be as one

And as they stared into each others eyes, removing the others mask, this was done

The music played on and they ventured together on this endeavour

For they knew in that moment, they would live forever

Though the fire around me raged like an unyielding storm

Over and over battering against my ship since the day I was born

Dive down deep below the sea to find

Something buried and awaiting to be set free inside

I look at you, the fire that tries to destroy my will

I say to you I have my own fire within that burns brighter still

So try as you might with your poison words and whispered lies

Like a phoenix emerging from the ashes I will still rise

For the divine spark living within me is a part of my whole

Don't doubt it, I am a girl with an indomitable soul

Down to the stream I venture at night

Through the firefly woods alive with the bright lights

A gentle buzzing in the air, vibrating within my very bones

Wayward eyes watching me from the grass, I'm not alone

Branches and leaves crack underfoot

Leaving a trail of my journey for those to come

At the water's edge I hear the call

A voice so pure and free, the sound cannot be heard by all

The flowing blue waters seem to welcome me

I greet them in return as if I have been here before, perhaps in a dream

Dipping my feet into the calm flow

Surrendering to that which is above and below

Staring into the clarity of the waters I see a face that is true

Somehow something was there that I knew

So strange and yet familiar this face I see before me

Every passing breath my heart skips a beat

I know I've seen this reflection before

Something inside is sparking alight to my very core

Years pass before my eyes,

Memories abundant light up the skies

A quiet laugh bursts from my lips as I come to see

That the face in the water smiling back, is me

Set sail,

Last night I dreamt a beautiful dream

I was flying through the sky it would seem

Over great rivers of flowing gold

Filled with secret treasures untold

Across the pink painted mountains

Hidden inside crusading water fall fountains

I reach the top of the ice

Enraptured by the beauty of the northern lights

I pull my boat and anchor into the starry sea

Close my eyes, deep breath in; believe

Set sail, set sail, set sail

I know where I'm going, somewhere without time

To search for undiscovered dreams and claim my freedom, this is the sign

Farewell, I will see you again traveller of your dreams

Away I go into the distant story of the never-ending tree

Into the unforgettable journey, the unknown, the future, I shall not fail

Set sail, set sail, set sail

Hold out a light someone hold out a light

Light the lanterns and watch them take flight

Know yourself and smile

Enjoy this moment, hold on for a while

You are eternal my darling

As sure as the water in your spring

Listen to your heart tonight, he will not betray you

All along it was meant to be this way and all along you knew

Sometimes I wonder about things I do not know

Sometimes I wonder when will they say go?

To see the world in all its glory

To have adventures and tell my story

Every night from my window I see the clear blue sky

As I wait for the mysterious darkness, time passes me by

The sun of the day turns into night and the shining stars take flight

I wonder perhaps great people of the past live in the light

Do they see us as we fly our kites?

I dip my feet into the cold stream

I wonder does anyone else share my dream?

Do they close their eyes and get swept away?

Do they live their lives by every day?

To live a life worth living, a life worth taking risks for

Take the opportunities as they knock on the door

I wonder what will happen tomorrow

Will it be full of joy or full of sorrow?

Who's to say what will happen today

So live your life in your own way

I don't know which moment will be my last

So no regrets don't live in the past

The wind in your face, your dreams by your side

Open your eyes, open them wide

Climb every mountain and face your fears

Wear a smile, show no tears

Learn from your mistakes and when you get knocked down get back up again

The things I believe they make me free

I wonder what will my life turn out to be?

Will they see a different figure or will they see me?

Follow your heart, stand up tall

Live life to the fullest or not at all

Trust yourself and you will find

Sometimes the heart speaks truer than the mind

I wonder, do we choose our paths or do we have our destiny?

Is the future written in stone or planned out for you and me?

I wonder every single day,

I wonder if the thoughts I ever wonder will stay

I don't want to wonder all my life so from this day forward

I will strive to explore the world to the top and back around

For life is a journey that's homeward bound

Even when all other lights go out, the spark in you will not fade

For you my dear are a rare creature to behold, yes you were made

To light up the sky and bring your force of love to all you see

Deep inside your magic, you yourself are the key

So trust yourself, know who you are, do not doubt

The spark in you will not fade, even when all other lights go out

Sing the song of the music in your heart

Beating louder and louder from where you did start

Know this journey is filled with all you see in your mind

The power you have to start again and what once was lost you now find

You are a complete manifestation

One from your own depths of creation

Still one question remains above all that is here, now, answer true

To yourself you must ask and you alone can answer: who are you?

And like the flower that blooms in spring

She will once again begin to sing

The sweet melody of magic and love

That flows in her veins from the sea above

A smile upon her cherry lips dancing and playing

Her words will entrance you in a heartbeat no matter what she is saying

Look into those emerald eyes and be swept away

Into a world of legend and adventure, come what may

Try to touch the waves of her golden hair flowing like the sea

Get too close to her pulsing heart and you'll be

Chemically changed from that moment until forever

A part of her story in the book she has created together

With all forces of this world entwined like the veins of a giant oak

Glimpse of her magic and you are eternally woke

Who is she really this girl made of stars?

What secrets stir beneath her heart?

Will you ever know the truth about her mystery?

Anything is possible in this world we live in

You may find her alone in a forest under the night sky

She'll be staring up at the stars wondering why

Why she is the only one, the journeys been far

And her heart will be light and her eyes will fill with stars

Don't stop dreaming darling

Under the water all is still

Holding your breath tight in your lungs until

That very moment when you break the surface of the blue

Holding life and death in your grasp, it's you

Warrior, adventurer, believer, you control your fate

As you breath in the air you realise it's never too late

To turn the tide around

And follow your path with your sound

The sound of your heart beating to the rhythm of your own drum

You hold the power so now decide and it will be done

Her red lipstick marked a map all over his chest

A map that would lead him to a place of undiscovered dreams and the rest

Of the world would look on to the lights beyond the shore

Come with me now she said if you want more

If you want to quench the thirst you feel down deep inside

To discover the quest that is your destiny and in time

Find all that you have been called to see

For what you seek is also seeking me

This was foretold long before this time

Our souls are joined in ancient magic, here now, yours and mine

Dreamers are the fire that will light up the world

Whose hearts are pure and although sometimes they get burned

They will never stop singing their song

For they are driven to find the place where they truly belong

When the day comes when they ask me for the story of my life

I will turn to the woman inside

Who has taught me the power of courage in a world filled with fear

The power of trust that makes the path so hidden become clear

The greatness of wisdom from the wise

That makes you see everything with new bright eyes

Love is the song of magic that creates from the deep

To follow your destiny when you can no longer sleep

Every moment here is a piece of the game

And I in all my being am an eternal flame

So you ask me for my experience here inside

I tell you look into my eyes, there you will find

A tale two fold of adventure and choices of which I will not apologize

All I have done, is the ink on the paper of the story of my life

Fly away butterfly

To somewhere you can look each moment in the eye

Like the caterpillar that transforms inside the cocoon

Every flower has its time to bloom

Like the lightning that strikes at night

Every creature here has a chance to fight

Like the rainbow that appears after the chaos of the storm

Humans have the ability to recreate, to be reborn

Like the glistening of the seven seas

We can all be still in our own tranquillity

Like the sun that rises from the darkest hour

To light up the night, we all have that power

So fly away sweet butterfly

You are your own salvation, to yourself you cannot deny

She came in the night like a firefly

Lighting up her way as the time passed by

Took from me what I can only give

And in return gave me a reason to want to live

I await her presence every midnight

Out in the woods under the stars light

I will never forget the sparkling of her eyes

Oh how she came in the night, like those fireflies

Destiny is calling me

Into a journey of adventure and epiphanies that was always meant to be

Don't listen to the outside babbling of those around you

To your own inner voice you must stay true

For try as they might and try as they will

To bury your voice and ultimately kill

Your power that you have inside

Remind yourself who you are, do not hide

For you are the one alone that can sail your way

So to the voice within, you must never betray

Say to those cowards that which you have known all along

My fire burns ablaze, so strong

My own melody, my own song

Not a thousand barrels of water could subdue my flames

Burning forever, indomitable, that is my name

Come with me my sweetest friend

Over the bridge to journeys end

Leave this dreary world behind

You were born to do more than just survive

Rise up now and stand with me

Look to your heart and you will see

Spread your wings and let's fly

After all, they say dreamers never die

When the world is sound asleep

You remain awake, immersed in the deep

Day dreams dance inside your mind

Floating among the stars, leave this world behind

Venture to the endless sea

Forever and ever you'll be

All your life you've known

And when you feel the spark ignite inside

You wonder how you lived before this time

Your own fire breathes and comes to light

This is your journey, your life, your fight

Power seething in your bones

Yes that feeling, you've always known

Now light up the sky with your eternal flame

Write among the stars your true name

Hearts beating in the night

Dreams dreamt float away and take flight

Where do all these stories go

Somewhere over the rainbow?

Who are you really voice in my head?

Will you remain when all is done and said?

Dreaming my life like a writer

Does knowing this make my burden lighter?

In the night when I yearn to fly away

Through the tears you will always stay

Whispering ancient songs of love and forever

My conscious mind with me on every endeavour

Old soul, you know with certainty

Who I am more than me

She closes her eyes to see her dreams

She knows nothing is as it seems

Locating the ember in her mind

To start the revolution of this time

All who see her in this trance

Know this is the beginning of a life long dance

For now she knows her mission

Opens her eyes and oh how they glisten

This is the ultimate quest of mine

Open my eyes and oh how they shine

And at the end of it all who would believe her?

This golden girl, fearless, a pure dreamer

The sparkle in her eyes, the vibration of her being

All she is, so pure, to know her is freeing

He looks at her and she looks at him

To tell their story where would she begin?

"Write about us" he whispered into the wind

"You know I will" she answered as she grinned

And in that moment their eyes did gleam

And with a piercing glance spoke 'I'll see you in my dreams'

The eyes are the window to the soul

No truer words have ever been told

And at the end of it all you will find her at the edge of the world

Writing in her book

Smiling to the world

And her eyes will fill with stars

To be near her

Was to taste adventure

And touch destiny

She was as fierce as they come

With a hint of magic in her eye

Her name will be known until the end of time

And her legacy will never die

Down the path of no return

Walking into the sunset

Leaving all her troubles behind

To her new life she looks ahead

And welcomes all moments of magic

Oh darling, all the magic is within you

Your eyes could light the sky

Beauty of mine

My love for you will never die

For all the wonders of the world

You are the rarest of them all

Nonpareil in spirit

Never have I known another

Be true now, who are you girl?

She took my hand

To ride the winds and back again until the end of time

Are you with me?

Are you a dreamer?

I'll never forget the smile that lit up the world

Under the shine of the stars amongst the vastness of the desert

Bursts of colourful light shot into the dark sky

And at its source is a girl, dreaming of a life coming soon, sending out her signal fire

Even as their piercing eyes longed for her to fall

She did not waver

And even as the world around her darkened into shadow

Her light remained brightly shining

For she knew there was something alive and pulsing inside her that would burn forever

She turned to them and smiled

There was nothing in this world

That could quench her fire

She is the brightest star in the night sky, lighting up the darkness

As she spoke, her voice just above a whisper

She raised a glass to the darkness

Embracing her fate

"To the ones who dream"

She knew the journey was waiting for her, beyond all the forgotten dreams, the lost hopes, the bittersweet loves, there lay a way for dreamers

I'll meet you in the whispers of a fairy-tale, under the bright lights of ideas, in the tears of dreams lost, in a world forgotten but resting on the slightest glimmer of hope, to be remembered and once again brought back to life

Midnight city

How curious your twinkling stars

How enchanting your infinite darkness

How different the night

How alive the buzzing fireflies

I welcome the twilight of this world

Through all the magic of this time

Through the howling of the lone wolf

Through the silent breeze between the trees

Through the whispers of spirits at the water

Under the stars that gaze upon me

Under the never-ending mystical force

I know in my very core

I feel more myself than ever

You've got the music in you

Rare soul indeed

The light that shines in your eyes

Like a sea of stars in the darkest night

Even in day light

Her spirit will wander

Into another place, another time, another dimension

Untamed, wild and free

Walking the Earth until she comes home,

To the place where the lonely ones roam

Call her a fairy and she'll fly away to another land, leaving pixie dust in her path

Call her a mermaid and she'll swim across the deepest oceans, leaving a trail of bubbles for you to follow

Call her a wide eyed wanderer and she'll walk the Earth in search of her truth, leaving a trail of bread crumbs for others to follow

Call her magical, adventurous, stardust made, one of a kind, ethereal

But if you dare call her ordinary

You will fly, swim, walk across this world with the undeniable and unending feeling that there is something more out there waiting for you,

The same thing that is already within this magical, adventurous, stardust made, one of a kind, ethereal girl.

Drink of your sparkling water

Swallow deep the mysteries of this life

Until they become with you one and the same

Pour into the river your hopes and dreams, your secrets and desires, your deepest thoughts and your memories closest to your heart

Drink up my dear, drink plentiful

Drink until the end of time

Then you raise your glass and wake up

Because it was all a dream

One last time can we run down the hill and feel the wind in my hair?

One last time can we midnight dip into the pool of dreams and feel alive in the dead of night?

One last time can we stare up at the sky wondering why and feel infinite amongst the Gods above?

And always we will feel magic in this story of love

Dear me, don't leave this world without igniting the magic inside

She stared at herself in the mirror

Gazing deep into her sparkling eyes and smiled

She is magic

She is her own woman

Something had changed within her

Something had sparked a fire inside her soul

And now, the fire burned ablaze inside her heart

Her stories returned to her

And she would never forget them

For she was, is and always will be the eternal fire

You could tear off my wings

And I'd still find a way to fly

My melody is coursing through my blood,

My heart pumping to the beat of my song

And I'm dancing to the rhythm

And then you feel it…

The power, the magic, the energy around you is in tune with your soul and the universe is in sync and the whole world is with you

Every soul has her own song

Sometimes you find another's song that matches so perfectly with your own that you know you were made for each other

And you can't hold back the tears

Tears of joy having remained true to yourself

Tears of sadness when you know this moment will never be as it is right now

Tears are droplets of pure feeling made real in this world

I'm lost

Lost in a world where fairy-tales no longer ignite magic

Lost in a world where stories whispered around the fire no longer reach the strong of heart

Lost in a world where poems no longer strike courage into the hearts of men

But one day soon in the wheel of time, I will journey homeward bound

Sleep easy do I, knowing that someday soon, I am found

Come meet me by the river under the cover of darkness

Silent steps approach

Who are you stranger

Who visits me in dreams that may or may not be mine

To you I speak now

Come meet me under the stars above

I will tell you a story

I will be true to my heart

Dream about me tonight

I need a place to rest my head

Dream a dream of timeless romance

Dream of a quest filled with adventure and courage

And when the wheel chimes at midnight

I'll meet you there, in your dreams

I often wonder about my adventures in my past lives

All leading to this moment

Now

Oh what a wonderful game is life

Remember all those bedtime stories you knew when you were young?

They're real

Sit with me a little longer friend

Let us dream of rainbows and unicorns

Let us dream of waterfalls and mountains

Let us dream of oceans and beaches

Sometimes the dream is more real than real life

What story makes your heart beat a little faster?

She took it back, her power, but then she never really lost
it

You recognise your own magic in others, with just a glance, somehow you know

You'll find your way through the darkness when you become the darkness, you let it in, you surrender, and only then will you blaze across the sky, only then will you become the fire and oh how you will burn, burn forever.

Wanderer, vagabond, king of the journey

Travelling to distant lands

In search of yourself

A road map to the stars etched across your heart

You leave lanterns on the cobbled stone way for those who come after you

Though we all have our own path

Sometimes they cross and we meet our match headed in the same direction

Don't look back dear one

Legendary times lay ahead

It's meant to be

I'll meet you in the Promised Land

What deep secrets a woman's heart carries

Lovers, lust, nights of passion, nights of despair,

Moments of strength and moments of weakness

Memories, hopes and dreams

Beauty remains

She may choose to share her secrets with a man if he has touched her heart

But some secrets, she will not whisper a word of to another breathing being

The secrets meant only for her to know until the end of time

They remain locked away

Buried inside a chest that lives at the very bottom of her ocean

The sparkle in your eye never fades

You are capable of anything

Now, look inside, all the answers are there

You've always had the power and always will

It was you all along

Now fly…

Oh how I search the night skies for you wandering star

Magic encases me

Darkness surrounds me

You've been there all along

Now I see

We found each other's gaze across the camp fire,

Eyes meeting, sparking a ripple through the very fabric of this world

One look was all it took

Electricity ignites in my bones

Sparking a revolution inside my core

I stared at my comrades who remained after it all

Twirling my hair around my fingers

I spoke clearly the words of all the dreamers that came before us

To live the dream would be the greatest adventure of all

I know who I am

I know why I am here

I know where I have been

I know where I am going and no one will stop me

Because I know

Be brave darling, courage of the heart is so rare in this world

I hear the owl hooting in the depths of the dark woods, and just like the wolf that howls at the moon, I relate to his call, his echoing sound in the eternal silence, his shot of light in the blackness, his signal fire to alert his blood, his call to the wild depths of his soul

I'm so in love with the night

Her dark mysteries of legends old

Her shining stars of souls

Her absolute beauty

Her whispering call to wandering souls

Another world of enchanting wonders

You will always find me

Alone at midnight, tears streaming down my face

Mind dreaming of a story untold

Gazing whole-heartedly at the night and her treasured stars

I created a world of my own inside my head and I go there often

To my destiny, I'll meet you there

All through the night I wonder why the stardust in my soul creates such sweet melodies as I dance to the beat of my heart. And I know I am magic.

Waters filled with stardust

Twinkling and shining

As I dip my feet into the cold embrace

Magic caresses my body as I fall into the water

Pure euphoria

Forever you will stay in my heart

As I stare up at the stars you are all I see

Her kind will never come around again

I hear the call from the nightingale singing sweetly at dusk

I hear the call from the owl hooting lonely at midnight

I hear the call from the wild lions roaring at golden dawn

I hear the call from the wayward wanderer whistling a tune as old as time

And I recognise the call, for it is mine also

And I realise all are we on a winding path searching for ourselves

Dreamers in this world

And on our journey we meet those who share the same dream

I've found that when you know how to play the game, it's actually fun

I feel like I'm bringing it home

And in the thick darkness when you are on the brink of giving up

You hear a voice calling to you from the wilderness

Serenading your soul

You have a nostalgic feeling that you know this voice

And you're pulled back into your being

Knowing that you won't just survive, you'll truly live

Because that voice belongs to someone with mighty power and divine spirit

And all will be as it was meant to be

For the voice calling to you in the darkness, is YOURS

Am I the only one awake in the early untouched hours of the morning wondering about my whole being?

Am I the only one singing quietly to myself at midnight hoping that my lullaby will bring me solace?

Am I the only one searching for adventure in this existence?

Am I the only one listening to the birds song and the winds whistle as I venture into mother nature?

Am I the only one dreaming of fairy tales and moments that make my heart beat faster?

By the hidden smiles, the glistening eyes, the faint expression of hope in the faces of strangers I see,

I know that in this crazy world, when each time I imagine myself in a story of my making in which I am on a quest to find my true self, somewhere out there is another with the same thoughts and I can smile knowing that I'm not the only one

It goes beyond that now, this is about

fulfilling the destiny of my soul

Written in the stars

A legend in my heart

Wander along the path of dreams

My magic will ignite the spark

Your heart knows

As she looked back at this adventure of a lifetime

She couldn't help but stare up at the night sky and smile

Her story is legend and will forever be known

In the fabric of this world her tale has been sewn

Trust, wisdom, love, loyalty and courage bound to her being

Now she sees come to life all she has been dreaming

Forever she'll hold close to her heart

The faint whisper of hope that's been with her from the start

And in the end it was do or die

Eternal and indomitable, The Girl With The Star In Her Eye

He watched her, as with every beat of her heart, she was grateful for the infinite sparkles of magic within her.

"Lets live forever." She whispered

"What do you seek?" He asked "Something only I can give to myself." She answered

Sparkling magic dripped from her lips as she spoke the
ancient words,

telling a story to the stars above her,

who listened to every breath she took

To breathe her in was to inhale her magic and destiny, now her life of adventure would always be within you

These are the nights,

The nights when the fire burns bright in our sparkling eyes

The nights when our feet are covered in dirt from running down to the lake

The nights when tears of joy are streaming free down your face and you let them flow

The nights when the stars are so bright in the darkness you believe with all your heart that they are shining just for you

The nights when we feel the magic of this world pulsing all around us, so close we can almost see through the veil

The nights when we look at each other and we know that right now is the most precious moment that there ever is

These are the nights when I know I am alive and I feel infinite

These are the nights

I still hear the song of my youth,

playing soft melodies in my ear,

melancholy music,

sometimes I wonder if the little girl I once was will be proud of the woman I have become

She had that twinkle in her eye

And mischief playing on her lips

You could imagine her

Dancing naked under the stars

While the campfire blew embers

Saluting her great unyielding love for life

My darling, there's a voice inside your head for a reason

Down the road of no return,

I'll meet you where the fairies dance in ponds of starlight

Look up at the sky and smile.

This dream we are dreaming is pixie dust under our wings so lets fly…

"Lets go on an adventure" she had said one day,

and I knew she didn't just mean today,

she meant for the rest of our lives

Lets lose ourselves in the pure and undeniable magic of this world.

In the vast woodlands of fairies and all mysterious things. In the beckoning darkness of the night as she calls her stars.

In the winding roads less travelled, leading to the way out of this labyrinth.

In the afterglow of dreams lived and all explored.

In the setting sun, the sky on fire with deep colours that resonate with your very being.

Yes, darling, lets lose ourselves in the pure and undeniable magic of this world.

"So we meet again"

"I always knew we would, that our paths would cross once again"

"I see you've picked up a few scars along the way"

"As have you. But we're both still here"

"Indeed we are"

In the darkest nights,

come to the edge of the whispering woods,

across the bridge above the still river,

you'll find me there, waiting.

And so, the story goes on…

How magical it is, that words on a page can change your life as you know it

Darling, this is it

Away I go, journey into the land of sweet dreams,

into the imaginary realm where all stories appear in my mind,

sometimes I look for you there in my deepest dreams, amongst these eternal stars,

I've known you since the beginning

In this strange life if we do not meet for a time along our paths of fate, I know without any doubt, I will see you in my dreams.

Land of dreams beckons me

When will I wake from this sleep?

Lucid dreaming tonight

Dreamers are legends and legends never die

Tell me the story of your life.

The story of the wanderer who's lived many a times before now,

Look deep into my eyes and whisper the words you've been writing into the fabric of this world for eternity.

Then I will know that this is it.

Put your hand on my heart and feel how it beats for you.

Feel how with each pump of my blood, my veins sing to your soul.

Beating to the rhythm of our love, echoing in eternity.

Lets watch the sunset until the end of time,

oh how I feel alive

Soft lips on mine, embrace me

I know, even if my world is falling down around me

    I will rise from the ashes and start again

    for my soul is pure and will live forever.

Somewhere deep in the forest there's a pool full of dreams that I visit at night now and again.

How the waters glow like fairy dust, swirling as the stars twinkle.

How I seep into the waters only to rediscover lost dreams of the night.

Lets jump into the whirl pools that lead to other realms of reality,

lets climb snow capped mountains and breathe in the view of this magical world,

lets fly through the star lit sky and drink the star light

I knew the song you were singing before you even opened your mouth

Sail your ship into dangerous waters,

battle against all the monsters of the deep and return to your course with a few scars

new found wisdom and an unforgettable story to tell

Leave a candle in the window my dear,

like a lighthouse in the wildest storm,

your fire will call me home

Dance to your own song my darling,

how beautiful it is to watch your body move to the beat of your heart

Lets go back to the nights we'd sneak out and skinny dip
in the lake,

floating in a sea of stars,

drowning our worries,

feeling infinite among the Gods as we whispered
forbidden dreams to each other.

My kingdom awaits in the depths of my heart,

And I've come back home to myself

I see you in every blazing sunset that sets the sky on fire

I see you in the dark of night in-between stars that light up the sky,

I see you in my dreams,

haunting me until finally… we meet again

And as I stared into those large green eyes,

gazing into her sparkling soul,

In that moment I knew, she is the infinite magic

Smiling at her courage, heading towards the horizon

My blood drips into the stream below

Like sweet honey

And as I gazed into the waters of my youth

I saw a story of stars and alchemy and adventure

You thought I was dead but I have come back alive,

you don't know I have died many times inside but still I'm alive,

reborn again and again, resurrecting from the ashes of my former self, I am alive and now I'll fly

I felt myself come alive in the thunderstorm,

struck by lightning I felt the electricity awaken the spark in my blood,

coursing through my veins, this ethereal energy forever in my bones.

"What happened to that young girl with a heart full of dreams?"

"She woke up, but don't worry she's still a dreamer"

What is said in the dark is not often spoken of in the light

And if all the lights go out,

you'll still find me venturing through the darkness on the quest that I was born for.

And as they glared into the chaos of the wreckage,

they were not surprised to witness the girl emerging from the devastation,

not only having survived but fiercely alive and fire dancing in her eyes

The fire that burned within is fading to embers

but still you can set alight the sparks and become wild once again

Walk with me in darkness and you'll never yearn for the light again

Through all my adventures,

I have never felt more alive than when I saw your soul through those glowing green eyes

Every moment that is not spent with you becoming more alive and your heart being set on fire is the deepest betrayal.

Trust your soul, she knows.

When destiny knocks on your door, welcome it, for it won't knock twice.

Wrong, it will knock forever,

but when we have become who we are meant to be all along,

it won't have to knock

I'll wait for you forever my love

Come, let us dance in the meadows of our youth as the sun sets once again,

then at last in darkness, we will be home.

Our world is filled with stories, so what is yours?

Kiss me before its too late

I knew you long before I ever met you

I see the same spark in you

As powerful as the ocean is blue

So dive down deep into your being

You must know and feel without seeing

Rise again from the ashes and go forth on your quest

Walk your own path this is the best

Adventure and great knowledge await ahead

Become alive, no longer one of the dead

What is meant for you, you will always find

Look to your heart, for it speaks truer than your mind

Swift winds are rising

Look to the horizon

Destiny fills the air

Faster than the speed of a midnight hare

Come out to play this game you know so well

You're dreaming now in this place we call hell

This time in the wheel of life you will not fail

Trust yourself and look within, you will prevail

There's a power in the words you speak and the songs you sing.

You can create a whole world from the ashes of nothing.

The magic is within you

Deep inside I know this much to be true
You possess all the power you need
Now go forth and plant your seed
Into the Earth it shall grow
Until the time approaches when you shall know
The reason you were born into this realm
You are the captain of the ship, take the helm
Stormy waters are not kind
This dream you are dreaming is all in your mind
You've carried that feeling with you from the start
Have no fear, trust only your beating heart
Immortality is waiting my friend
At last we will reach the end
Of this story that will become legend
Down the path of no return
Into the fires as we ignite and burn
From the fires we shall rise and be
The dreamers, dreaming eternally
But now to the stars we journey
To infinity I can see the star lit sea
Home is where the heart is, that's what they say
I have thought about this moment every day
Now I can see
all along the magic was within me

Lets venture into forbidden forests and get lost so we can find ourselves

Only welcome the true and those who have courage of the heart

Those who gaze at the stars

Are the true dreamers

Stories are upon us, around us, within us.

When you tell your story let your voice be enchanting and your words be true

Her blood ignited the electric spark and her stars shone bright,

this was the path that would lead her home, the path of her heart

My stars shine brightly in my eyes

Stardust glows in my veins

I am my own darkness

And I am my own light

Listen now for the owls call, for he is wisest of all

We sat under the stars that night, drinking whiskey and toasting victory as the blood from our battle wounds trickled along our bodies of flesh, and as the singing of the warriors faded into the black night, we two were left and I stared at her, my love, the girl who had become a woman before my eyes, still she gazed ahead into the darkness, few and far fires signalling the reach of our battle. "Turns out these are the stories I was meant to tell" she whispered, knocking back the whole bottle of whiskey and closing her eyes as she flew to the land of dreams

The gaze between strangers is very peculiar, as for that fleeting moment your souls acknowledge one another and you wonder if you have ever crossed paths before, in another time, in another life

The fire is alive within you. I see the flame dancing in your eyes. You are so utterly alive.

Dive down deep into my dreams tonight, you know the way, even if your mind has forgotten, your heart remembers.

You must not let the dull buzzing of every day life lull you into a fatal sleep, block out that false sound, only listen to the eternal song of your beating heart

I was a warrior once, fighting in battles to reclaim ancient lands. Blood drenching the ground beneath, that was then. I'm still a warrior but now I fight a battle between minds, the strength of will inside, I will not falter now.

Love yourself first darling

I whisper ancient secrets from my memory to the mountains that touch the sky. I tell them my stories. I ask them about the mysteries of life. One day I'll hear them answer instead of my echo like thunder in the sky. Perhaps I already do.

Run, run away now while you are still you.

My lips are thirsty for the taste of you again

Just when you think it's over, when all hope seems lost to the void, that my dear, is when you truly find out what you are made of, that is when the magic happens

Tales of romance and broken hearts are my favourite because for a heart to truly be broken the love must have been real…

Unicorns, ancient creatures of nature and starlight, I knew you once, when you walked the Earth, now in the stars above, you gallop across the night sky, I will see you again, oh legendary friend of dreamers.

Late night drives with nostalgic music, no inhibitions and a sense of legendary wonder

Sail your ship to where none have gone before, or if they have none did return to tell the tale…

Dance with me now, dance with the music in your blood
and the song in your soul

Smile, because you know that no matter how hard they try to take away everything around you, to break you down, to make you submit to their will, you know with all of your being they will not kill the spirit inside of you. So smile and let your smile say "you have no power over me"

An echo from the song I used to sing

Come back to life

And so the adventure begins

All through the night I watched the sky light up with colours of green and red, dancing to her song, to her story, all through the night

A bittersweet moment this will be. For our journey together will forever be in my memory. We have shared thoughts and dreams. We were meant to meet so it would seem. Let us not say goodbye for we have too many tales to tell. Let us look each other in the eye and merely say farewell…

Taste of your blood in my mouth as I swallow a part of you, your life now inside me and forever will be

Your voice sang melodies in my ear, ancient songs long before I heard you speak

Look into the water, ever flowing, submerge yourself in the waters of youth, then will you know your truth

A fairy so pure and bright. Alive in places where dark meets light. Sprinkling fairy dust in natures home. Feel their magic in blood and bone.

A message to all the writers and poets out there. I know you feel alive when you take pen to paper. Getting lost in your dreams and imagination. You are the grand architect of your own creation. Exploring worlds and characters that stem from your heart. You were born to tell stories from the start. So write, and write the song that sings in your blood and bone. Write all the stories that make you feel like you are home.

Tell your secrets to the mountains. Tell your dreams to the stars. Tell your fantasies to the ocean. Then, maybe you will tell yourself how magical you are.

Ocean waves, adrift in your embrace, carry me to distant shores where I may rediscover lost dreams

Travel in the darkness of night, there under starlight will the shadow of this world reveal itself

Deep into forests I venture in search of something that does not in this realm exist

Your story my dear, is legend among dreamers

Walk through the fire. Flames dancing to the song of my heart. Dancing were the flames in my eyes. Igniting the eternal fire in my soul. And in the darkness of night I emerged from the flames. Alive, indomitable, the eternal fire

Beauty remains in the hearts of those who had the courage to start again

Sing your song my darling, those with pure hearts will hear the melody.

Someone once asked me how I tame the fire inside me, I smiled and answered, "I don't, I leave it wild and free"

Love is the magic we can feel with every fibre of our being

I welcome the night and all her stars, she is the one who knows all my dreams

Something about an open window, gazing out at the stars above, night fast approaching. Dreamers sat at the window staring up at the sparkling sea. All you wandering souls. All you dancers under the starlight. Lets climb out our windows and run away into the night.

Darling, your heart knows and has always known. Now do you have the courage to listen?

I see a beauty so bright in your eyes

Lets fly away to a midnight world filled with stars

Power resides inside those who believe in the magic within their hearts

Lightning Source UK Ltd.
Milton Keynes UK
UKHW040210031220
374527UK00001B/221